Home is Where You Hang Your Heart

A Mother's Devotional

by Cynthia Culp Allen

PRESENTED TO

_____

_____

_____

FROM

_____

_____

_____

Bite-sized meditations
to help mothers
through the crazy days.

MERIDIAN®
SLIMLINES

To my children,
who gave me these stories,
and to Charles,
who gave me the children

M33 Slimline Gift Edition

ISBN 0-529-07135-5

Book and cover design by Gayle Raymer

A Meridian Publication

Published with World Bible Publishers

Manufactured in the United States of America

Contents

Preface

Cynthia Culp Allen was introduced to us through the Amy Foundation, which, in 1989, recognized her for her Special Santa Story, the last meditation in this book.

Amy Awards are granted to select authors who have an article published in the non-religious media, and who include in the story at least one scripture verse.

Cynthia's retelling of the miracle of another mother's Christmas so moved us that we invited her to compile these delightful daily meditations from her own life.

Here they are. Delightful. Inspiring. Moving. Reflective.

Several of these meditations have been published as articles in newspapers and national magazines. We've collected them here for your enjoyment.

Special appreciation is extended to Sharon and Cameron Wills for their Special Santa Story.

—The Publisher

Lord of Those Crazy Days

This is the day that the Lord has made;
let us rejoice and be glad in it!
Psalm 118:24

I had one of those crazy days—again. The baby was wailing, the kids were fighting over who would answer the phone, the teenager announced that she got a *D* on her history test, the preschooler drizzled honey all over the kitchen floor, and I stumbled over a toy as I rushed to answer a knock at the door.

I wanted to scream—and I would have if no one had been at the door.

But instead I composed myself and proclaimed, "Hang it all! We're going to the park!"

There, amid the peaceful setting and away from the clutter at home, we recouped from our crazy day. The kids ran until their energy was spent, the teenager studied her

history . . . and I sat under a tree by myself.
But not alone. The Lord sat next to me and
I complained to him about my crazy day.

*Lord, it's been one of those wild and crazy
days when I need you more than ever. What
would I do without you when stressful days
hit? I handle the peaceful, pleasant days just
fine by myself. Yesterday I thought I had life
all together. But your Word tells me not to
"boast about tomorrow for you do not know
what a day may bring forth."*

*No kidding! That's probably why you allow
these crazy days, Lord. Days like today send
me running to you for strength, wisdom, and
comfort. I manage to fill the saner days with
activities that squeeze you out of my hours.*

*But oh, Lord, I need you today. Right now,
in this very moment. Help me to remember
that every job has its occupational hazards.
These crazy days are a natural byproduct of
raising children.*

*Yet, you have promised me the power to get
through these days as you would live them.
Victoriously!*

*And you have promised me your presence,
every day of my life.*

*You've given me your peace. Not a peace
like the world offers, but a peace that will last
through ANYTHING.*

Power, presence, and peace. Your promises to see me through this life. Victoriously. What more could I ask?

Oh no, Lord, here come Carly and Caleb, squabbling. Could I ask for one more thing? Patience! I need extra patience on a day like today.

Power, presence, peace, patience. Your promises for those crazy days.

Thank you, Lord.

Dead Monkeys

*You will again have compassion on us;
you will tread our sins underfoot and
hurl all our iniquities into the depths
of the sea.*
Micah 7:19

Two-year-old Charity toddled into the kitchen and handed me a bent photograph.

"Yook, Mommy," she said, holding it up for me to see, "an uggy, dead monkey."

I burst out laughing.

"Honey," I informed her, "this is no dead monkey. It's you!"

Charity had brought me her hospital birth photo. You know, the ones that make all—oh, excuse me—*most* babies look like dead monkeys!

Fortunately, Charity grew out of the "dead monkey" stage and became a beautiful young woman. Of course, God knew all along that she would. He had planned every detail of a sweet, pretty girl named Charity before he laid the foundations of the earth.

Watching my children grow into beautiful, capable young adults makes me evaluate my own spiritual growth. Is my heavenly Father pleased with the way I am growing up? Have I moved out of the "dead monkey" stage? Am I moving toward "beautiful creature" maturity?

With the proper program—lots of spiritual nourishment from God's Word, the exercise of my faith, rest in prayer, and cleansing from sin—I am assured of growing into the woman God planned me to be. And thankfully, God promises to bury my "dead monkeys" in the deepest sea!

Father, I stand in awe over the perfect plan you have for each of our lives. Thank you for not letting our sin mar the beauty of your plan. Each day is new and fresh with you, Lord. You are ready to forgive and empower us to live the life that will please you.

Keep Paddling

Being confident of this very thing that
he who began a good work in you will
carry it on to completion until the day
of Christ Jesus.
Philippians 1:6

I'm sitting on the warm sand under an even warmer summer sun. My husband and children are playing in the waves, but I'm watching a young man in a kayak struggle against the rough surf.

Paddle, paddle, paddle forward. Back, back, back the waves push him. Paddle, push, paddle, push. His fight to move forward is unending. I watch him stroke furiously for over an hour, only to be tossed continually back into the foaming, shallow water. Now the break of a monster wave submerges him completely. Soon, however, he emerges, the sun glinting on the bow of his kayak. Undaunted, he is still paddling.

Sometimes in my spiritual walk I struggle to take two steps forward in my godliness, only to have circumstances knock me back three. At those times, I wonder if I'll ever make any forward progress.

Oh look! The man in the kayak has broken through! He's paddling strongly now, skimming smoothly, confidently, out toward open sea. His perseverance has finally paid off.

The lone man in the kayak gives me hope. If success is possible through his human strength and perseverance, surely I can expect God to complete his work in my life if I remain faithful to him and his Word. Someday I will reach my goal: to be like him.

Oh no! A huge wave just crashed over the top of me and my notebook. Blast it all, now I'll have to start this devotional over. Oh well, I now understand that perseverance is the key to victory. Let's see, where was I?

Lord Jesus, you promised to finish the good work that you began in my life when I accepted you as my Lord and Savior. When the waves of circumstances crash over my head and push me back into shallow water, keep me paddling! Help me to remember that there is a smooth sea on the other side of the next big wave.

My Eternity Pants

*There is a time for everything . . . a
time to be born . . . He has made
everything beautiful in its time.
He has also set eternity in
the hearts of men.*
Ecclesiastes 3:1–2, 11

When I was nine months pregnant with
my fourth child, I spent most of one whole
day catching up on a mountain of ironing.
Positioned as close to the ironing board as
my huge belly would allow, I was deter-
mined to finish the job. Several hours later,
however, my back ached and my veins
throbbed.

"Being pregnant makes everything
harder," I groaned, feeling like I would be
pregnant for the remainder of my days. A
glance at the pile of laundry suggested I
might also be ironing for the rest of my
natural life. Sigh. Some duties can be such a
burden.

I pulled a pair of my slacks over the

ironing board and began to press them. Chad, then eight, came and stood beside me, watching as I ironed.

"Mama," he asked, "are those your eternity pants?"

Eternity pants! The very idea lightened my weariness. Chad's mistaken name for my specialized clothing—maternity pants—expressed perfectly how I felt about my condition. But praise the Lord, all things come to an end. Mountains of laundry are finally moved, and babies come in God's good time. Only God's Word lasts forever. There is light at the end of every dark tunnel.

Thank you, Lord, for the hope you always provide just when I need it. When I grow tired and discouraged, give me strength and determination to see my earthly tasks to completion. I'm looking forward to my eternity with you.

P.S. Baby Caleb came that week!

Clean Stables

*He gives children . . . so that she
becomes a happy mother.*
Psalm 113:9 (TLB)

"I just cleaned this room," I grumbled to
no one in particular. I began again to pick
up scattered toys, crumpled papers, and
cast-off clothes. I had been cleaning house
all morning. I would get one room sparkling
clean, then head to the next. While I was
hard at work in that room, the toddlers were
busily destroying the room I just completed.

Nothing helps much. Logical arguments
about the virtues of neatness are met with a
blank stare from a peanut-butter-smeared
face. Spankings speak a commonly understood language, but there's the tiny problem
that toddlers aren't actually being bad, the-
y're just being themselves.

A right attitude helps. One night as I was
praying about never being able to keep
ahead of the housework, the Lord showed
me an odd little verse in Proverbs.

"An empty stable stays clean, but there is no profit from an empty stable," (Proverbs 14:4 TLB).

No, I don't live in a stable. And I'm not raising animals—although sometimes it seems both of these statements could be true!

But the principle is the same: I could keep the house clean if it was occupied only by little old me. But what would that profit me? I would be lonely, dissatisfied, bored. Laughter and activity fill the house because it is full of children. Sure, they make continual messes. But they also offer my husband and me joy and fulfillment. And children do eventually grow up and move out—leaving us alone in our empty stable, uh, I mean house.

I need to enjoy them NOW. Maybe we'll go to the park this afternoon. We can swing and slide and play tag. That way the house will stay clean for several hours. But first I better go straighten up the living room—again!

Lord, thank you for making me the happy mother of children. Help me to enjoy them in these young, messy years. Help me to place my priorities on important things, such as introducing them to you.

Home Is Where You Hang Your Heart

Behold, I will be with you always . . .
even to the wilds of L.A.!
Matthew 28:20 (Cindy's version)

Several years ago, my husband came home and announced, "Hon, it looks like we will have to move to Los Angeles."

I was horrified. I had enjoyed a rural life in northern California for many years. It seemed as if a part of my relationship with God was wrapped up in the quiet country-side. How could I have my daily prayer-walks without peaceful scenery? How could I move to the "Big City" with its crowds, traffic, and smog!

"I certainly hope not!" I answered. "Los Angeles is the worst place God could ask me to go. But I will pray about my attitude, in case it's his will for us."

So I began to implore God to work on my attitude. It amazes me how he can change my heart to fit his plans. By the time we had to move, I actually wanted to go!

If we are willing to give up our own plans, and even some dreams and desires, and submit to God's will, we can know what God, the Almighty One, can truly do.

I no longer feel that my security is in a place or a people. My security is in the Lord. And he is with me in all his greatness and love, wherever he leads me to go. After all, God is the same God here in Los Angeles as he is in northern California!

Lord Jesus, I have peace in knowing that you are with me, wherever you ask me to go.

You have accompanied me to many cities and countrysides, to various states, and even a few foreign countries.

You were the same Lord and friend to me there that you were back at home. I can trust you to always be there for me.

Super Friend

Greater love has no man than this, that
one lay down his life for his friends.
John 15:13

The television blared at its loudest pitch.
So did my three-year-old's holler.

"Super friends, Mama!" Caleb yelled
from the living room. "*Super Friends* are on!"

I shook my head. That kid knew all the
latest heroes: Ninja Turtles, Dick Tracy,
Super Friends! With three older brothers
and sisters what did I expect?

Still, it bothered me. Every day I read
Caleb a Bible story, often using flannelgraph
to keep his attention. We talked about Jesus,
and to him, throughout our day. And Caleb
looked forward to Sunday school each week.
So why did he remember the world's heroes
better than the amazing characters from
Bible times?

Sigh. I needed to pray more for Caleb. His
brothers and sisters already had an exciting
relationship with Jesus.

I went in and sat next to Caleb on the floor in front of the television. Wrapping my arms around him, I asked, "Who's a real Super Friend, Caleb?"

"Batman?" he asked, his eyes never leaving the show.

"No," I answered.

"Robin?"

"No."

"Superman?" Caleb wondered, turning to look at me with wide, puzzled eyes.

"No," I said, laughing at his expression. "Jesus promises to always be Caleb's Super Friend!"

Caleb returned my happy squeeze and looked back at his show.

Jesus, you have always been my very best friend. I can confide in you like no one else. You are faithful and trustworthy. You support me, accept me, and believe in me. You give me the help I need every time. And then there is your unconditional, sacrificial love for me.

I know you want my friendship too. Help me take the time to be a friend to you. And to remind Caleb about your friendship every day.

City Lights

*Pay attention to the Word of the
Prophets, as to a light shining in a dark
place, until the day dawns and
the morning star rises in your hearts.*
2 Peter 1:19

A week after we moved to Los Angeles
from northern California, I stepped into the
backyard one evening for some time alone.
Looking up at the night sky, I couldn't see
even one star!

"I know the stars are up there," I said.
"This is the same sky we looked at last week
in northern California. The stars are there,
the lights of the city are just obscuring their
light."

This realization made me think of the
huge city with its many distractions: streets
lined with shops and businesses; fast-food
eateries and restaurants; theaters; schools;
and flashing neon lights everywhere urging
people to stop at every one.

Life everywhere, not just in Los Angeles,

is full of distractions that block out God. Yes, he is still there—always the same, unchanging, steadfast. But we are unaware of his presence because of everything else competing for our attention.

Still searching the sky for stars, I prayed, "Lord, you have brought us to this place through your clear direction. Please keep us committed to daily quiet times with you. Help us to practice your presence in the midst of the city's distractions. Let us shine with your light here in this darkness of unbelief."

Just as I finished my prayer I saw one tiny star blinking way up in the yellow sky.

Lord, we've lived in L.A. for over a year now and our lives are still bright with you. Thank you for being faithful. The city's alluring distractions don't satisfy as you do. Keep lighting our days with your truth.

The Power of the Cross

For the message of the Cross is
foolishness to those who are perishing,
but to us who are being saved it is the
power of God.
1 Corinthians 1:18

Early in our marriage, my husband and I lived with and cared for my ninety-year-old great-grandmother. During that year, Grama and I attended a Bible study together.

The other women and I would drift into lofty philosophical discussions—the really "deep" stuff! We enjoyed debating heavenly matters. But then, out of the blue, Grama would pipe up with her quavering voice and mutter something about the Cross of Christ.

At the mature age of twenty-one, I considered her comments quite childish.

"Oh bother, Grama!" I thought, "nothing like sticking to the superficial stuff when we're moving on to the deep insights, the really important issues of Christianity."

Time went on, my dear Grama passed on, and I finally grew up. Through the Word and life's circumstances, the Holy Spirit taught me the lesson Grama had already learned. The Cross of Christ is most important! Embodied in it is the freedom to be all we can be in God's image, the mystery of redemption from sin, eternal salvation, and the great love that we all long for.

Grama, positioned so much closer to eternity than I, could see the significance of the Cross of Christ. Its truth overshadowed every other: Jesus Christ loved me enough to endure the agony of the Cross that I might be saved for an eternal relationship with him.

Thank you, Lord Jesus, for what you suffered on Calvary for me.

Thank you that I grew up enough to realize the power of the Cross.

Thank you for great-grandparents, grandparents, and parents who knew and taught this great truth.

I love you, Lord!

Prescription for an Ailing Tongue

I have resolved that my mouth
will not sin.
Psalm 17:3

Like a fool, I passed along the gossip as carelessly as a kid playing a game of telephone.

The juicy tidbit made its rounds and came back to me. The person it was about confronted me.

How sorry I felt that I had hurt her and destroyed the confidence she had in me! I wanted to take back every word. But I couldn't. We never can. I had to be responsible for what I had said. I asked my friend's forgiveness—and the Lord's.

Still, I had one more apology to make. I hurried over to the friend's house with whom I had discussed the matter in the first place.

"The Bible says we're to confess our sins

to one another so we might be healed," I explained. "I'm here to do some confessing . . ."

A few instances of obeying this verse cured my "wagging tongue syndrome". Like the common cold, however, it's a recurring ailment, so I'll always keep the Divine Healer's guaranteed prescription handy.

Lord, you made our tongues, and you have a purpose for them: to praise, to bless, to edify, to encourage, to witness, to speak the truth in love.

Like David, I have resolved that my mouth will not sin. Set a guard over my mouth, O Lord. Keep watch over the door of my lips. And if any evil escape, remind me to take my medicine—confession to you and others—so I might be healed.

Nothing Is Bigger Than Jesus

Behold, I am the Lord, the God of all flesh; is there anything too hard for me?
Jeremiah 32:27

"Mommy, that mountain is really big, huh?" asked four-year-old Chad. "But not bigger than Jesus!"

When Chad was little, he would often direct my attention to the enormity of a tree, skyscraper, or mountain. Then he would always assure me that each object was definitely not bigger than Jesus.

How big is Jesus? I wanted an answer to this question, and I found some special truths in my search.

Our Lord is a great God (Psalm 95:3). His Hebrew name, El Shaddai, means God Almighty. Jesus is omnipotent—he has complete power. This power includes the creative power he used to create the universe; also, the resurrection power that we trust in for salvation.

God never needs to refuel like we humans do. We understand limited resources and shortages, as created beings in a created but fallen world. But God never experiences an energy crisis!

Our God is infinite—he has no limits or bounds. He cannot be measured. We modern-day worshippers entertain too small a view of God. Like my son said, God is big!

Chad's simple, trusting attitude rubbed off on me. This trust in an awesome God flooded my heart with peace before major surgery. It carried me through several years of serious illness. Jesus was bigger than these. He was with me in all of his greatness and power.

The next time difficulty towers, stand strong and remember my small son's lesson: nothing is bigger than Jesus!

Lord, what comfort and strength it brings me to focus on your greatness. Thank you for simple, trusting children who teach us some of your deepest truths.

For His Eyes Only

*My mouth will speak in praise of the
Lord. Let every creature praise his holy
name for ever and ever.*
Psalm 145:21

My third pregnancy ended in a miscarriage. What a disappointment! We had tried for over a year to conceive that special baby.

Sitting in my hospital bed afterward, I pondered the whole situation. After almost four months of pregnancy, all I was left with was a horrendous headache, a fat belly, and a big, fat hospital bill!

I asked the usual questions—all of the "whys." "Miscarriage" sounded so much like "mistake." Did God really know what he was doing? Why would he give a little baby life in the womb, only to take life away before the child took its first breath?

My mind drifted back to a book I had read not long before: *Perelandra* by C. S. Lewis. Lewis created an imaginative and unusual world in which lived some extraordinary creatures. My favorite was an animal (I think—only Lewis could describe this one!) with jet-black fur. It lived high in the deepest woods. The creature sang a continual song of praise, hauntingly beautiful and melodious, with its head turned upward toward heaven. It didn't sing for the enjoyment of people. The creature had never seen or been seen by a human. The sole purpose for its life on earth—and its song—was to praise God.

Aha! I thought. Could this be the "why" I was hoping for? Perhaps those little babies, unseen by human eyes and miscarried for whatever reason, were God's praise. Created solely for him—to give him pleasure and praise.

Sigh. The thought helped me feel somewhat better. I laid back on my clean, white pillow and was able to fully rest.

Lord, your glory is more than our human minds can comprehend. It can only be satisfied with praise—praise of the purest kind.

Make me a creature of praise, not one of show for others' eyes. But a creature of praise for your eyes and ears only.

A Heart Transplant

*Christ bore our sins in his own body on
the Cross, that we, being dead to sin,
should live unto righteousness; by his
wounds we are healed.*
1 Peter 2:24

"Organ transplants!" The an-
nouncement on a morning talk show
flashed across my television screen. It wasn't
a very appetizing subject to accompany
breakfast, but the topic intrigued me.

Two couples met in a television studio to
discuss their personal experiences with
organ transplants. An animated man
laughed and talked of how he had received
a donated heart. Each beat of that heart,
courtesy of someone else, kept him breath-
ing, laughing, talking, living.

Next to him sat a quiet man and woman.
Their teenage son was the donor of the other
man's transplanted heart.

The man with the new heart continued
talking. He shared his life-changing experi-

ence when he visited the grave of the boy whose heart now kept him alive.

"I realized then that someone had to die so I could live," he said, sobering for the first time. Shaking his head, he added, "What a cost."

Unable to contain my thoughts, I exclaimed to the man on television. "You're right! Someone did have to die so you could live! It was Jesus Christ. He willingly gave his life for you. If that teenager could have chosen, his choice would have been life for himself. But Jesus Christ chose to die to guarantee life for you."

I continued my conversation with the tube, "Oh, mister, I wish I could tell you personally. Jesus *can* give you a new heart— one that will go on ticking for eternity. I don't mean the flesh and blood heart you're concerned about, but Jesus will renew the very heart of your being, the eternal spirit that is you!"

A commercial break came, and I got up to clear the breakfast dishes. My day was off to a great start: I felt a fresh commitment and gratitude for the person who had willingly given his life for me.

Lord, you bore in your own body my failings; you were weighed down with my sorrows; you were pierced for my transgressions and crushed for my sins; the punishment that brought me peace was upon you, and by your wounds I have been healed.

Yes, what a cost! Thank you, Lord.

Deep Roots

May your roots go down deep into the
soil of God's marvelous love.
Ephesians 3:17 TLB

My husband and I stood in the backyard watering our recently planted lawn.

"Looks good, doesn't it, Hon?" I commented, surveying the wide expanse of three-inch-tall green.

"Well, it *looks* good," my husband replied, pointing the hose toward a dry corner, "but I think we're going to have to replant it."

"Replant it! Whatever for?" I asked.

My husband spoke from years of experience in growing things. "The new grass grew up too quickly and it doesn't have a root system strong enough to support it. It will all die soon enough."

He was right. We had to replant.

A few months later I had a conversation with our friend Richard Wheeler, an evangelist. In my excitement about all God could do with Richard's unique ministry, I began spouting off ideas as fast as they came to mind.

"Whoa!" Richard stopped me. "I don't want my ministry to grow faster than my character!"

Wow, Richard knew the same secret about growing spiritually that my husband knew about growing grass: deep roots equal strong, lasting growth.

Since then I have prayed, "Lord, don't let my ministry grow faster than my character." As my life is watered daily with the Word and my character is exposed to the light of the Son, the fruit in my life grows strong and sweet.

Lord, I don't want to be like the shallow, rocky (hard-headed and hard-hearted?) soil in your parable. No depth in my life. My roots not deeply planted in you. Then when trouble comes or time marches on, my enthusiasm fades and I drop out.

Help me to grow to be like you.

The Voice of Authority

Encourage and rebuke with all authority.
Titus 2:15

If you have children, you know the scenario. It's a work day at home. You've assigned the children their chores and have begun to tackle your own, but soon you hear trouble brewing at the back of the house.

Finally an indignant six-year-old marches into the kitchen and tattles, "Mom, Chad won't help me clean the bathroom!"

I turn to look at Carly and know she's telling the truth. Her older brother isn't pulling his weight.

"Tell Chad that his job is to help you clean the bathroom," I review the orders.

"I've tried to tell him but he won't listen to me," Carly complains.

In my firmest voice, I command, "Tell him I said so!"

A smile brightens Carly's face. Happy to oblige, she runs to quote (and embellish) my message.

The voice of authority! No matter which one of the kids needs prodding, it always works!

Perhaps I could apply the "voice of authority" principle in my spiritual witness. Sometimes in a discussion with friends I'll try to throw some spiritual light on the subject. Invariably, someone will ask, in effect, "Who says so?"

If I know my Bible, I can answer with full assurance, "God says so!"

God is the ultimate authority.

Like Carly, we can march into battle with confidence that we have a voice of authority behind us every step of the way!

Lord, thank you that I have the strength of your Word supporting my faith in you. Help me to always speak confidently, knowing that your voice of authority never fails.

A Childlike Request

*If you, then, though you are evil, know
how to give good gifts to your children,
how much more will your Father in
heaven give good gifts to those
who ask him!*
Matthew 7:11

I was asking God to grant me a most outlandish request, and small, nagging doubts drowned out my wishful prayer.

"How can you ask God for something so big? You've told people about your request. What will they think when you don't get it? It will make God look bad and you look stupid!"

And yet, even as I mulled these negative thoughts over in my mind, I knew my giant request was one that God could use to glorify himself. I also knew that through it I could become a more qualified servant of his.

I had analyzed my motives and they were pure. The dream remained. So I kept asking—and slightly doubting—until I read Matthew 7:9—11.

The verses reminded me of a time when our family was shopping in a thrift store. Five-year-old Carly had fallen in love with a mangy-looking doll. Her desire for the doll gave her the courage to ask her father for it.

"Can I please have this dolly, Daddy?" Carly pleaded, holding the weathered doll for him to see. Her dad gave the doll a quick glance. He had one thing on his mind: finding camping gear for a week-end trip. Instead of telling Carly an immediate "no," however, he placed the doll in the shopping cart, hoping she would forget about it. At the check-out counter, he set the doll aside. Soon, he was packing bags of camping stuff into the back of the car.

On the ride home, Carly leaned forward, gave her dad a hug, and sweetly said, "Thank you, Daddy, for buying me that dolly."

My husband and I exchanged looks. He made a reckless U-turn and headed back to the thrift shop. A few minutes later Carly was hugging the dolly that only she could love.

Carly was well aware that her daddy had the ability to buy her that doll. She also knew that he was in the habit of giving her "good gifts." Carly *expected* that her father would grant her this reasonable request. So much so that she thanked him for it without actually having it in her hands. Just trusting that it was already hers.

Carly's request, her expectancy, and her thankfulness won her that doll!

Lord, help me to have an expectant heart—knowing full well that you have the power and desire to grant me my requests that are good for me.

An All-Wise God

*"For my thoughts are not your
thoughts, neither are your ways my
ways," declares the Lord. "As the
heavens are higher than the earth, so
are my ways higher than your ways
and my thoughts than your thoughts."*
Isaiah 55:8–9

Today one of the five-year-olds in my
Sunday school class taught me something.
After singing our choruses, marching
around Jericho more than seven times, leap-
ing into the lion's den, and rocking for forty
days in the ark, it was finally time to settle
down for a Bible story.

The lesson was about God's great wisdom, and we were talking about how it was
demonstrated through creation.

"I know God must be wise," little Isaac
interrupted. "He has about a thousand
heads!"

I'm not sure where Isaac got his theology
(possibly straight out of his five-year-old

imagination). But he's correct in his matter-of-fact certainty about God's wisdom.

When we closely inspect creation, whether the universe or the human body, we are convinced that it must have come directly from the hand of an All-Wise Creator.

As we watch God at work in our lives, the perfection of his ways points to a mind far greater than ours.

We can trust God's Word when he promises that our Lord and Savior is full of wisdom. We can trust him to take complete control over our lives.

Lord, I am so thankful that your wisdom far exceeds mine. I can rest in the fact that you are great enough, wise enough, and good enough to take care of me and my world.

A Fishing Lesson

*"Come, follow Me," Jesus said, "and I
will make you fishers of men."*
Mark 1:17

Our family was spending two relaxing
days in a tiny fishing village on Mexico's
Pacific coast before heading back to Guada-
lajara to finish our summer Spanish course.

One of the village men had taken us
across a lagoon to a jungle island for a
dinner of fresh, grilled fish. As we sat under
our thatch-roofed cabana enjoying our dinner, we watched a young man, browned by
the sun, catching fish with a net.

Into the water, he tossed the big net.
Then, only a moment later, with a pull, pull,
pull of the big net, out came a large, thrash-
ing fish. I was amazed at the consistency of
the fisherman's luck.

"Maybe it's not luck at all," I thought.
"He seems to know some secret about fishing that I could afford to learn. Jesus called
his followers 'fishers of men.' Perhaps I

could learn a spiritual lesson from this man's earthly trade."

The first thing I noticed was his huge, untorn net (can't have any holes to let those fish get away!). Is my method of soul-winning effective, or does it need a bit of mending?

Another obvious trait was the fisherman's consistency. In went the net, out came the catch—time after time after time. To catch fish, he knew he had to get the net out of his hands and into the water. The only way to catch people for Christ is to get the Gospel out of my mouth in the first place—time after time after time.

Finally, the fisherman seemed to know the perfect spot to catch fish. When he had caught all there were to catch in one place, he rowed to another spot and began to catch still more. I know I need to go where the spiritual fish are. I'm certainly not going to catch them drifting in my Christian currents all the time!

One night Jesus' disciples fished all night without catching a single fish. Jesus suggested that they throw their nets on the other side. After some argument, they finally obeyed. The resulting catch was so immense, it tore the net! Spirit-directed evangelism is always the most effective!

Lord, you promised to make us fishers of men. I have experienced the unique joy of "fishing" with you to bring others into your kingdom. I want to know this joy on a daily basis. Help me to be faithful, to be bold, and to be sensitive to your leading.

Looking Up

*For the Lord himself will come down
from heaven with a loud command,
with the voice of the archangel and
with the trumpet call of God. . . .
Encourage each other with these words.*
1 Thessalonians 4:16, 18

One of our favorite songs at home is the peppy chorus, "This is the day, that the Lord has made." We really get into it—loud, lively singing complete with enthusiastic clapping.

Caleb, our three-year-old, loves to sing it too. But he has his own version, which we hear him singing at the top of his lungs while he plays in his room.

"This is the day, this is the day, that the Lord come down, that the Lord come down. I will rejoice, I will rejoice, that the Lord come down, that the Lord come down."

We all smile at each other when we hear Caleb singing "his song." But even as I laugh I wonder, "Isn't he right? Shouldn't I begin each day reminding myself that this could be the day that the Lord Jesus comes for his children? Doesn't the Bible tell me to rejoice and look forward to Christ's soon return?"

During an earlier stage of my Christian life I lived each day with the expectancy that Jesus might return that very day. What excitement it brought to my days! The thought comforted me in times of trouble. It also intensified my witnessing as I tried to "redeem the time."

I believe I'll follow Caleb's leading. Each day, I'll remind myself that this might be the day that the Lord "come down" for his children. And I'll rejoice in it!

Jesus, I can't wait for the day of your return! Help me to keep expectantly watching for you, to keep looking up!

Service With a Smile

And my God will meet all your needs
according to his glorious riches in
Christ Jesus.
Philippians 4:19

My friend was telling me about his desire to be a missionary. Normally, I don't question the call of someone to the mission field, but my friend's call to the Caribbean seemed somewhat unusual. All he talked about was the beauty of the islands, sunning on sandy beaches, the tropical climate, scuba diving, and seafood. (You know, the real inconveniences that showed his willingness to suffer for the Lord!) But he never mentioned people.

"Do you have a burden for the people in that part of the world?" I asked.

"Not particularly," he replied, unconcerned. "Maybe that will come later. I just think it would be fun to live there, and that would give me a good excuse!"

Hmm, the fun in serving God is not in the location, but in being obedient to God.

I will pray for my friend and trust God to change his heart. The Holy Spirit can give him the right reason—the desire to share the Good News of salvation and fellowship in Christ—for going to the mission field.

But I also know that God can use us—even when our motivations are wrong. In the past, he has used me in spite of myself. And I'm not the only one. Look at Jonah. He certainly had the wrong attitude when he finally obeyed God and went to Nineveh as a missionary. And yet God used Jonah's angry preaching to bring the rebellious Ninevites to repentance.

Actually, God could do his work without disobedient servants—and have an easier time of it, too! But he chooses to use us, often in spite of ourselves, so we may share his joy now and his glory in the future.

Thank you, Lord, for opportunities to serve you, to share your glory, and to prove your mercy and compassion. Thank you for giving us everything we need to perform your work, including a proper attitude.

The Nagging Truth

A friend loves at all times.
Proverbs 17:17

One of my close friends had a habit of constantly bringing up my faults. I'd either end up apologizing for them or making a joke about myself. I couldn't understand why she couldn't accept me as I was—the good *and* bad. I appreciated her as a person and overlooked her personality flaws.

Finally, I complained to my husband. "If my friend doesn't quit nagging me about my unforgivable offenses, it's going to ruin our friendship."

He didn't have an answer for me so I turned to prayer and God's Word. Soon I found a pertinent Scripture:

"Love forgets mistakes, nagging about them parts the best of friends," (Proverbs 17:9 TLB).

I decided to share this verse with my friend at the next opportunity.

"You and I are growing to be close

friends," I said to her. "To be even closer, we need to learn to accept some things about each other. In some ways, you and I are as different as night and day. I like that aspect of our friendship, though, because it helps me see life from a perspective other than my own. I accept and appreciate who you are as a person, even where you differ from me. I hope you can feel the same about me." Then I shared the verse I had found.

You know what? It worked! The love of Christ has covered our relationship to this day. We are still very different in many ways, but we have learned to appreciate our differences. My friend and I enjoy a friendship as close as sisters. And of course, we are sisters in Christ!

Father, you want your children to live in the same harmony and oneness that you and the Son share. Help my friends and me to cover each others' sins with the blood Christ shed for all of us.

Dirty Ovens and Other Accumulated Sins

On this day, atonement will be made for you, to cleanse you. Then, before the Lord, you will be clean from all your sins.
Leviticus 16:30

I have a confession to make: I hate to clean my oven! I do manage to keep a tidy (yet comfortable) house, but my oven is one thing I don't seem to get around to often enough.

When an oven isn't cleaned on a regular basis, an overwhelming amount of charred crust accumulates. (Isn't that why the manufacturers put a door on the contraption?)

At one point, my oven got so bad that every time I baked anything our fire alarm blared, which would set off a chain reaction. The toddler would scream, making the baby wail, causing the dog to shoot out the back door like a torpedo, causing the older kids to comment, matter-of-factly, "Mom's baking again!"

Needless to say, I didn't bake often! When my children balked at my offer to "bake" yet another batch of "Rice Krispie Treats" for a bake sale, I knew it was time to conquer my dirty oven.

On my knees surrounded by cleaning supplies, I scrubbed, scraped, and scoured. Hours later, it still didn't shine quite brightly as I had hoped, so I continued my cleaning.

As I worked, God spoke to me. "This oven is like your heart, Cindy. Cleaning an oven shouldn't be this difficult, but you've let it get out of control. Like the sin in your heart, the longer it sits there, the harder the buildup is to scrub off."

I thought of my sins: resentment, unforgiveness, criticism, gossip. They were accumulating in my heart like the charred, black remains in my oven. And like the screaming fire alarm, there had been warnings.

My Christian service wasn't as effective as usual. And like my bake sale contributions, my ministries were of the half-baked variety, cooked up by little old me and not by the Holy Spirit.

I realized, working on my knees, that I was in a good position for confession. My cleansing did not require hours of work like my oven. The blood of Jesus Christ, shed for all of us, is a powerful cleanser. I was sparkling clean and ready for use after a moment of repentant prayer!

Lord Jesus, thank you for taking away the stains of my sin. Your shed blood cleanses my heart whiter than snow. I am eternally grateful.

Obedient Children

Everyone has heard about your
obedience, so I am full of joy over you.
Romans 16:19

Don't you love it when you ask one of
your kids to do something and he or she
actually does it?

If your children are like ours (normal),
they have days when they just can't bring
themselves to cheerfully obey.

Other days, it's "Okay, I'll do it. I'll be
done playing in a minute."

Then there are those few glorious occa-
sions when you call a request from the
kitchen and you hear, "Yes, ma'am."

What? What did he say? Did I hear right?
Yes, he said, "Yes, ma'am," and with such a
sweet, respectful tone of voice. Oh, I love
being a mother!

I especially love motherhood when my
three-year-old is in this agreeable mood.

He'll answer me from his play with, "Yes,
your Majesty!" (He heard that on a cartoon!)

Does my heavenly Father see me as an obedient child or as a willful one? When he asks me to do something, do I grumble and complain? Do I put off his request, making him wait on me?

There are times when I know God must smile because he asks me to do something and I answer immediately, "Yes, Sir." Or better yet, "Yes, your Majesty!" I am much happier when I respond to him that way.

Father, sometimes it takes your discipline to convince me to be an obedient child. Help me to remember that an obedient child is a happy child. Let me always answer you with a cheerful "Yes, Lord."

Emergency Surgery

*The Lord binds up the bruises of his
people and heals the wounds he
inflicted.*
Isaiah 30:26

Carly had an infected finger from a splinter, and I knew minor "surgery" would have to be done. With myself as surgeon and a sterilized needle as a scalpel, I probed and poked until I removed the festering sliver. Carly screamed and squirmed in agony through the ordeal, her face as red as her infected finger.

It pained me to hurt her, but I knew the "surgery" had to be done—for Carly's good. Before her finger could grow healthy and useful again, the infected splinter had to be removed.

A week later, Carly's finger was in perfect working condition. The miracle of healing had taken place.

I shared this illustration with a friend who was going through a trial. She knew the trying situation was God's intervention in her life. He desired to bring her back into perfect fellowship with himself.

I had experienced a similar situation. The Lord had to do surgery to remove an infected attitude that had burrowed deep into my heart. It hurt when the Holy Spirit used a situation and God's Word to cut into my soul and drain out the infection of sin. Like Carly, I cried and squirmed at the Great Surgeon's hand. But soon, healing took place and I was spiritually healthier than ever.

Holy Spirit, thank you for the healing that only you can produce in my life. Fill my heart with more of the Spirit of Christ that I might grow even healthier.

Little Leaguers and Lessons on God's Love

For great is your love toward me.
Psalm 86:13

If you have an athletic child, you've probably acquired a routine as regular as the seasons. Football, basketball, baseball, and swimming, that is. You sit on rock-hard bleachers in all types of weather, stretching your neck, looking for that one special child—yours! He (or she) may not be the team's Most Valuable Player, but he is doing his best and you're proud.

After the game, no matter what the outcome, you search for your child and wrap him up in a huge hug.

"Good game, Son," you praise him. "I could tell that you played your best."

At a concert, I heard Bob Bennett sing a song about how his dad came to all his Little League games. Bob was a lousy player, but "none of it mattered after the game, when my father would find me and call out my name," he sang.

I thought about the "Game of Life." When it is over, I will meet my heavenly Father face to face, and I will forget about the game just finished—the misses and mistakes, the falls and turned ankles, the remarks of the other players. I will be absorbed into his welcoming hug and his warm praise, "Well done, daughter, my good and faithful servant."

Bob finished his touching song with this line: "He loved me no matter how I played."

Thank you, Father, that you love me "no matter how I play." With the same degree that you love me today, you loved me as a newborn baby, when I could only lay there, small and helpless, surrounded by your unearned love.

I love you, Lord.

"Hooray! I'm a Servant!"

*The Son of Man did not come to be
served, but to serve, and to give his life
a ransom for many.*
Matthew 20:28

When Charity was small, I was the janitor of our church. She would accompany me on the day I cleaned "God's house" and help with the small tasks like dusting and taking out the trash.

I wish I could say she loved it, but some days Charity would rather have been anywhere else. One day she was especially disgruntled over having to clean with me. She came over to where I was mopping and, with wide eyes, asked, "Mommy, is God really for real?"

I leaned on my mop and assured her that God is the most real person she will ever know.

Immediately, she snapped, "Well, if he's real, why can't he clean his own house?"

Clever thinking! Why not? Of course, he could if he wanted to. The Almighty had cleaned up the chaos of the world at Creation. Why not clean his own house? Child's play!

Then I remembered another time that Jesus had done some cleaning. I told Charity about it:

"In Jesus' day, because of the dusty roads and sandaled feet, a servant would meet visitors at the front door and wash the dirt from their feet. One night Jesus and his disciples attended a banquet. They needed their dirty feet washed and there was no servant to do it. Do you know who washed the disciples' feet?"

Charity's eyes were wide again as she shook her head.

"Jesus washed those dirty feet. Jesus became their servant. Even that lowly job was not below him, and he was a King. But he loved his disciples and he could show them his love by serving them."

"Charity," I said, "that's why God allows me to clean his house. He wants me to know the joy of being a servant. And I'm glad to do it because this is one way I can show Jesus that I love him."

I continued my cleaning that day, and for several more years, but Charity did not continue her complaining.

Thank you for the opportunity to serve you by serving others. Lord, I am grateful for your example in servanthood.

An Important
Little Word

And the words of the Lord are flawless,
like silver refined in a furnace of clay,
purified seven times.
Psalm 12:6

When Chad was five, he would ride his little two-wheeler beside me as I jogged down our county road for exercise. One afternoon Chad was troubled about the weekly children's Bible club he attended.

"Mom," he said as we moved down the road, "we have to say a Bible verse at club and they make us say a bad word."

Hmm, I thought, what bad word could possibly be in a Scripture verse taught at Chad's Bible club?

Upon questioning, Chad was reluctant to tell me the offensive word.

"Are you sure I won't get in trouble?" he questioned.

"Of course not!" I assured him. "I asked

you to tell me, so it's not the same as saying it and meaning it."

"Well, okay," he began, "the verse is John 3:16."

Now he really had me wondering!

Chad continued, "The verse goes, 'For God so loved the world he gave his only begotten Son that whosoever believes on him should not perish *but*.' There it is, Mom. They make us say it!"

I chuckled to myself and marveled at Chad's tender conscience. Then I gave him a lesson in homonyms.

Because Chad pointed out that little word, I noticed the *but* for the first time myself. It was strategically positioned at that spot in the verse to show contrast. And what a contrast that verse contained. The difference between darkness and light. That little conjunction separated eternal destruction from eternal life.

Scripture is packed with concepts containing that threatening word:

Not worry *but* peace.

Not sadness *but* joy.

Not hate *but* love.

Not fear *but* faith.

Chad proved to me that I can have quite a Bible study with one little, seemingly insignificant, word.

Thank you for the Bible, Lord. I am grateful for each and every word contained in the Scriptures. They point me to you, show me what you are like, and assist me in learning your ways.

Help me to obey every command and expression that you have given.

Paid In Full

If you, O Lord, kept a record of sins, O Lord, who could stand? But with you there is forgiveness; therefore you are revered.
Psalm 130:3–4

I went eagerly to check my post office box. My prayer group had been praying that I would be granted a scholarship to attend a week-long writers' conference. I swung the box door open hopefully. There was an envelope from the conference director! After ripping it open, my eyes moved immediately to the conference fee column and to the big letters that said: PAID IN FULL.

As I slid into my car, I was praising the Lord for his latest miracle.

"Why are you saying that?" my four-year-old asked.

"Because Jesus just did something special for me," I answered.

Her face brightened. "Is Jesus in the post office?"

Laughing, I told her, "Yes, Jesus is in the post office when we need him to be. He's involved in even the smallest details of our lives."

My loving heavenly Father had provided not only my needs but also my desires. It was as if the Lord had reached down and wrapped me up in a warm hug.

I had been struggling, earning, saving to have enough money to attend the conference. Then someone unknown to me had paid my fee completely. I didn't have to do anything but go and enjoy.

Once, I had another debt—a horrendous debt that I would never be able to pay off— the overwhelming debt of my own sin.

I worked hard to pay it off, but I couldn't make any progress. Then along came Jesus and made one payment. Praise the Lord! Next to my name in heaven's account book, it now reads "Paid in full." Jesus Christ paid my debt completely. And it cost him something precious: his own life.

Jesus wants me to simply enjoy his blessings. I will. And I will be eternally grateful for his gifts.

Jesus, all I can say is "thank you." Thank you for being in the post office. Thank you for being on the cross.

Art 101

*For those God foreknew he also
predestined to be conformed to the
likeness of his Son.*
Romans 8:29

I love it when my children bring their art
work to me. Their proud smiles tell me how
they feel about their finished piece before I
even see it. Then I take the "masterpiece"
and form my own "unbiased" opinion.

"What a wonderful drawing!" I say. "Let
me hang it on the fridge where everyone can
enjoy it."

Artistic talent requires practice and a
good example to follow. I once took a tole
painting class, and while I was painting I
kept one eye on the teacher, the other eye
on my work. I watched the teacher's every
move and tried to imitate her. I studied her
finished pieces and tried to paint mine
exactly like hers. Actually, I copied her.

No, my painted pieces never looked just
like the teacher's. They never could—even

if I were as good as she was! My personality comes out in my painting (sometimes that is unfortunate!). But little by little, stroke by stroke, as I tried to copy my teacher, my paintings got more and more like hers.

In my relationship with Christ I'm taking a lifetime class in the art of being Christlike. As he teaches me, I keep one eye glued on him. I try to imitate him. Studying his Word helps me know his thoughts and actions in different situations. Jesus painted the whole New Testament with a broad sweep of love, forgiveness, and mercy. My prayer is that my life will be the same as his.

Lord, thank you for your promises that you will continue to conform me to your own image. Through your Word and the Holy Spirit's transforming power, I will someday become like you. My part is to keep my eyes fastened on you to see what you are really like. As I come to know you, I will become more like you. Help me to remain faithful in the art of becoming Christlike.

Putting Pretty
Into Practice

*Do you want evidence that faith
without deeds is useless?*
James 2:20

Charity is a perfectionist. In every area of her life she has a high standard of how things should be. When she was younger, she applied her perfectionism to her bed. She always wanted it to look picture-perfect: the spread smoothed, the ruffly pillows fluffed and positioned just right, her stuffed animals placed exactly so.

One morning, I went to awaken Charity and found her asleep on top of her spread, a blanket pulled over her.

"Why didn't you sleep in your bed last night, Charity?" I asked.

"I didn't want to mess it up," she replied sleepily. "It takes so long to get it just the way I like it."

"A bed is for sleeping in," I told her, "not

just to sit here and look pretty. What good is a bed that you can't sleep in?" Still shaking my head, I left her to dress.

Charity's perfect but unused bed is like a lot of Christian lives. Pretty, but useless. God wants us to be holy and righteous, of course, but also to be his instruments, his servants. Like a lovely porcelain cup, we should be clean *and* usable. Filled. Overflowing with God's Spirit.

What good is a pretty bed that isn't used? What good is an attractive Christian who is not available for God's service?

Lord, please clean me, polish me up until I shine like you. But then use me! Don't let me set on a shelf like a decoration, looking good but having no use. Let my life count for you, Lord!

A Tiger by the Tail

You will know the truth, and the truth
will set you free.
John 8:32

I love cartoons almost as much as my
children do! One of my favorite cartoon
characters is Mr. Magoo. As he nearsightedly
fumbles and bumbles his way through life,
he gets into the most outrageous predica-
ments.

In one episode, Magoo mistakenly put a
collar and leash on a tiger that had escaped
from the zoo, thinking it was his kitten. Off
they went on an afternoon jaunt through
the neighborhood. Mr. Magoo yanked that
bewildered tiger all over town until finally
the tiger came to the end of his rope (in
more ways than one) and Mr. Magoo discov-
ered his mistake.

Too often I stumble along in spiritual
nearsightedness like Mr. Magoo, not realiz-
ing that I have a tiger in tow. I don't see

clearly enough to know that the thing I'm hauling around is about to devour me.

Anything I attach myself to other than Jesus is a tiger. He gave his life to provide me with salvation and an abundant life. My part is to let go of all the tigers of worldliness and grab onto him. "To all who received him, to those who believed in his name, he gave the right to become children of God" (John 1:12).

Praise you, Father! Once I was like Mr. Magoo, but now I can see. And my eyes are focused on you. Help me stay focused.

First Love

We love him because he first loved us.
1 John 4:19

Before dawn one morning, I went around to the rooms of each of my children while they were still asleep—that glorious state of cherubic inanimation that every mother loves! At their bedsides, I kissed each child several times and whispered, "I love you." Then I prayed for them individually.

Ten-year-old Charity woke up. Rubbing her sleepy eyes, she asked, "Mom, what are you doing?" surprised, no doubt, to see me fully conscious at such an early hour!

"I just wanted to show you in a special way that I love you," I explained, "and I wanted to pray for you."

Charity hugged my neck and said, "I love you too, Mom!"

Later that day as I was peeling potatoes for dinner, she came to me. Wrapping her arms around me again, she kissed me and said, "Mom, for a long time you've been so nice to me. It's really helping me."

"Helping you?" I questioned.

"Yes," she said, "your love is helping me to be good and do right."

I returned her warm hug and thought, "Yes, that's the way it should be. God's great love for me makes me love him and want to please him, just as a child wants to please a loving parent."

The love that we have for our earthly family and our spiritual family should be kind, unconditional, and demonstrative. Surrounded by that kind of love, each of us will have the courage and will to do right and to become all that God means us to be.

Thank you, Lord, for your unconditional, all-encompassing love. Help me to love others and encourage them to do good just as you do me.

Blessings for All

Bless those who persecute you; bless and do not curse.
Romans 12:14

One evening I returned home late from an upsetting church meeting. As I crawled into bed, I told my husband all about it.

"First, they were talking unkindly about Sue. Then when I tried to stick up for her, they turned against me and began criticizing me. But you would have been so proud of me! I kept my mouth shut!"

I knew my heavenly Father was pleased with the way I had handled the testing. I did not slander anyone and had refused to get involved.

Earlier, the Lord had done a major reconstruction in my heart. I didn't need to put someone else down to elevate myself. God's Word had shown me how valuable I am to him. (It had also made me realize that I am important to him, but not more important than others. We need each other, working in harmony, to fulfill God's plan.)

"I know this doesn't make it right," I continued, "but I know why they acted that way. Most of them are suffering from low self-worth and never feel like they measure up." Understanding them helped relieve my hurt; so did knowing that I had passed the gossip test.

Still, I knew I had to go one step further to keep bitterness from rooting in my heart. I had to stretch my spirit and give a verbal blessing to each one that had been mean to me. For a few of them, I had to pray that the Holy Spirit would give me a blessing to share with them personally.

The next day—Sunday—I was able to share God's love with each one. If my blessings to them didn't increase their joy, they certainly did mine!

Thank you, Jesus, for noticeable growth in my life. I know it pleases you, and my spiritual progress definitely encourages me. I hope it brings a blessing to the lives of many.

The Self-Taught Girl

*I will instruct you and teach you in the
way you should go.*
Psalm 32:8

For six years I have home-schooled my
children. Charity, our oldest daughter, is
now doing well in high school. Chad, the
next child in the line-up, is an attentive and
diligent student. Then there's my third student, Carly. After several weeks of trying to
teach her the ABC's and counting, I complained to my husband.

"Everything I show Carly to do, she says,
'I know that already, Mom.' 'I can do that,
Mom.' 'You don't need to teach me that,
Mom.' She's going to end up being our
self-taught child," I trailed off in defeat.

I didn't push Carly that year, but I prayed
a lot and tried to allow her time to mature
and become teachable. And during that
year, the Lord spoke to me about the way I
had learned some of my lessons. I recalled
times when the Lord had tried to teach me

his ways and I had brushed him away with, "I already know that, Lord" or "I can do that; I don't need your help" or "You don't have to teach me that, God."

Then I had plunged ahead, doing things the way I knew how to do them. Like Carly, the self-taught girl, I ended up with my letters backwards and some of my numbers missing. But Jesus, patient teacher that he is, gave me time to mature and become teachable.

Thankfully, Carly is now learning the three R's. She even begs me to teach her other things, too!

Thank you, Lord, for the lesson I learned from Carly and for all your lessons in life. Teach me everything you want me to know, and help me to learn it your way.

Squabbling Siblings

Live in harmony with one another.
1 Peter 3:8

I know squabbling is natural in a family of several children, but I still hate it!

First, there's the blame:

"You used my _____ (fill in the blank)!"

Then come the angry justifications:

"Well, the other day without asking you borrowed my _____ (another item—equally unimportant)."

Next comes the criticism:

"You're just a selfish pig!"

Followed by a well-turned retort:

"It takes one to know one."

If I'm within hearing range, I make sure the squabble ends there. If I'm not, it could carry on to blows.

I don't see my children through rose-colored glasses. I know they were born sinners. But it grieves me when they treat each other unkindly. It's one thing to disagree. Quite another to come to blows, either physical or verbal.

I know our Father God feels the same way about his children. How he wishes we could get along with our saintly siblings. How it must grieve him when we don't! He doesn't expect us always to agree. Thoughtful people often come to different conclusions.

But our Father's desire is that we disagree agreeably. And that we concur on the one eternally important issue: that Christ loved each one of us enough to die for us personally.

There is no reason for sibling rivalry. Jesus made each of us with special gifts and abilities. He loves our individual personalities and wants fellowship with us on a solo basis.

Because of Jesus' sacrifice on Calvary, his children will live together for all eternity. It won't seem like such a long time if we get into the habit of getting along!

Lord, I know it pleases your Father-heart when I get along with your other children. Help me to live in harmony as much as possible. Make me a peacemaker.

You Can't Save Easter Eggs!

Give us this day our daily bread.
Matthew 6:11

I entered my daughter's bedroom armed with anti-dirt and anti-germ weapons: rags, ammonia, and pine-scented cleaner. My five-year-old wasn't yet proficient in room maintenance, and the awful smell seeping under her door told me that something—probably a mouse (I hate mice)—had died in there.

The smell was strongest near her closet door. Steeling myself, I threw the door open. My worst fears were confirmed. Her closet floor looked like the scene of a maggot convention where everyone had shown up! Gagging and trying to hold my breath at the same time, I proceeded to clean up the mess.

Finally, I found the culprit. Tucked into a dark corner was a plastic bag filled with rotting Easter eggs. This was May!

"Charity," I called, and she came running into her room.

"What are these?" I asked, holding up the disgusting things.

"My Easter eggs," she replied innocently. "They were so beautiful, I didn't want to throw them away."

I heaved the bag into the garbage can. "Honey," I sighed, "you can't save Easter eggs!"

The Old Testament tells about a group of people who tried something similar. The Israelites loved the sweet-tasting heavenly bread that God supplied daily, so they decided to save some, despite God's warning against it. But by the next morning their tasty manna had become a crawling, wormy mess.

God wanted the Israelites to enjoy their daily bread, yes, but also to trust in his provision for the next day, and the next, and the next. The people thought they had a better idea, however—to stock up a little security. But if they saved for themselves they wouldn't need to trust God, so God turned their manna into an inedible mess. In so doing he taught them a double lesson about trust and the consequences of disobedience.

Lord, let me enjoy your blessings each day, but don't allow me to "hang on" to them. Help me to let go of my past experiences, both good and bad, and move forward with you. I want to trust you to supply all of my needs each day!

Is Motherhood for the Birds?

A wise woman builds her house, while
a foolish woman tears hers down by
her own efforts.
Proverbs 14:1

Birds have taught me a lot about mothering. This is not to say, however, that motherhood is "for the birds!" On the contrary, I believe being a mother is the most noble of professions. It deserves society's highest respect.

One spring a little brown sparrow, as fat as a plum, built her nest in the oak tree just outside our window. My children and I, laying on our stomachs out of sight, watched her build her nest.

Bit by tedious bit, she collected her materials, picking something out of the thick grass with her tiny beak. Holding it tightly, she flew high into the old oak where her nest was already under construction. Down she would swoop for more materials; then back up to weave them into her nest.

"What is it that she keeps pulling out of the grass?" my daughter asked.

Looking through binoculars, I finally identified the mystery material. "Strands of the dog's hair!" I exclaimed.

We looked at each other in amazement, marveling at the ingenuity of the little mother bird. She knew what would make a soft, warm nest for her babies. And she was committed to providing the necessary labor to construct a proper nest.

Another year, a mother killdeer taught me what *not* to do in nest-building. Killdeers build their nests in rocky places, and this mother decided to make hers in the middle of our long gravel driveway. I spotted the small, speckled eggs in her flat, stick nest and warned visiting friends to drive carefully. In time, the eggs hatched into fuzzy, round chicks.

One day a huge dump truck rumbled down the lane to bring top soil. Afterwards I hurried down the road to the nest. It was crushed. The baby birds, flattened by the huge tires, were scattered here and there. I felt sad and disappointed.

"What a stupid mother!" I thought. "Doesn't she have enough sense not to build her home on a road. That would be like me telling my kids to play in the middle of the freeway!"

But the poor little killdeer had no way of knowing that not all rocky places are alike! Sometimes mothering takes wisdom far greater than our own instincts.

Dear Lord, only you can provide the wisdom I need for effective mothering and nest-building. You know us fully—my children, my husband, and our home situation. Give me personalized instruction and guidance. Help me put into practice the advice your Word offers. Holy Spirit, open my eyes to my blind-spots and empower me to build my house, not tear it down.

Learning to Say Thanks

I will give thanks to the Lord.
Psalm 7:17

One warm summer evening years ago my grandfather and grandmother took us grandchildren out for ice cream. As I sat in the back seat of the dark car on the ride home, I felt inner turmoil. I wanted to express my gratitude, but somehow it got stuck in my throat.

At last, my will won the struggle. I leaned forward and whispered, "Thank you for the ice cream, Grampa." He responded with a gracious acknowledgement that I will never forget.

"Cindy," he said, "if you will always remember to be thankful, you will bring glory to God and you'll be somebody special in life."

After that I said thank you as often as I could!

One time Jesus healed ten lepers he met along the road as he traveled to Jerusalem. In their excitement at being healed, they all rushed off. Only one of them turned back to say thanks. The Bible says, "with a loud voice he glorified God, and he fell down on his face at Jesus' feet, giving him thanks."

I wonder what made the man go back. Perhaps in his childhood his dear grandfather had taught him the importance of saying thanks!

Thank you, thank you, thank you, Lord. You have done so much for me, I can't say thank you enough. And I am grateful for parents and grandparents who taught me the importance of thanksgiving.

Tied Up in Tinsel

For it is time to seek the Lord.
Hosea 10:12

One afternoon near Christmas the mail-man delivered a large box.

"It's here, kids! It's here!" I shouted to my children. We'd been waiting for this package for several months.

We had ordered the "Rolls Royce" of reading programs. After much deliberation, I had narrowed the choice to two phonics courses: one was quality and twice the cost; the other came with a Treasure Chest full of tiny, plastic toys as reading incentives. I opted for the expensive one, rationalizing that my children were worth it.

Eight-year-old Chad and I tore into the big box and began taking out the contents. As I exclaimed over each piece, my son continued digging. When he finally hit bottom a frown crossed his face. "Is that all there is?" he asked.

"All there is?" I echoed, viewing the array

scattered all over the floor and remembering the two hundred plus dollars I'd spent on this "little bit of stuff."

"Where's the Treasure Chest?" he asked.

Then I understood. Thinking I had ordered the other program, Chad had been anticipating that Treasure Chest full of tiny toys. Now he was disappointed.

My expectations are a lot like Chad's. God offers me the very best in life, the "quality stuff," yet I desire cheap trinkets.

Ironically, it is during the holy season that I am most prone to filling my life with worthless trinkets: things that won't satisfy; that will be broken or lost by tomorrow; and that really aren't worth keeping anyway.

In the hurry-scurry of life I often make the wrong choices. Oh, my gift choices are correct; it's the decisions about how to spend my time, not my money, that I regret. I skim over the deeper, sometimes quieter experiences for the more frivolous activities that lure me to participate. Usually the quieter choices will be the most cherished: strolling silently in crisp-cold air and watching a creek bed fill with snow; singing carols and reading the Christmas story by firelight; kissing angels on Christmas Eve as I tuck covers under sleeping children's cherub-chins.

John Quincy Adams once told his daughter, Abigail, "Think of no other riches but those of the heart."

That's a thought I'll consider as I make this year's Christmas list.

Lord, this year all I want for Christmas is riches of the heart. I want time, not tinsel. Time to contemplate; time to make warm memories with those I love, memories that will satisfy and last a lifetime; and time to spend with you, the one whom the holiday celebrates.

Listen When You Walk

*My sheep listen to my voice; I know
them, and they follow me.*
John 10:27

The line of people waiting to see Madeleine L'Engle looked endless, but I didn't hesitate to add myself to it. In one hand I held her book *A Wrinkle in Time* for her to autograph for a friend. In my other hand, I clutched her book for Christian artists and writers. That one was for me!

At last I was face to face with Madeleine L'Engle.

"Please," I requested, handing her my book, "sign it with the most important advice you can give me as a Christian writer."

Madeleine chewed her pen thoughtfully, staring past the line of expectant people, past the building, out into some distant place of knowing. Finally she scribbled her advice in my book, closed it, and handed it back to me.

"I really think this is most important," she said with an assured smile.

I thanked Madeleine and hurried away to read her advice.

Inside the front cover she had written, "Cindy, listen when you walk."

That's perfect, I thought. Most of my mornings begin early with an hour-long walk spent praying, meditating, and listening to the Lord. I get some of my best writing ideas during that time.

But this advice applies to much more than my writing ministry. It works for my Christian life as well.

As I have learned to quietly listen to my Savior's voice, I have come to know him and his ways. It's a step-by-step journey—a walk, if you please—into deeper fellowship with Jesus Christ: to know him is to love him is to worship him is to serve him is to glorify him.

This is my prayer for myself and each dear one in my family. And now, as I end this book, it is my prayer for each reader as well.

Lord, may every reader come to know you as Savior, Lord, and friend and follow you step by step. And remind us all to "listen when we walk."

Special Santa Gave the Gift of Prayer

For human beings this is impossible,
but nothing is impossible with God.
Mark 10:27

As I pulled from the hospital parking lot I wasn't expecting anything special to happen. The day seemed like all others. Every day I made a trip to the hospital for my three-year-old child to get his radiation treatment. Every day when we left the hospital we passed the Santa in front of the flower shop on The Esplanade. And every day Cameron asked to see him.

Today was no exception.

As I pulled onto the street, the shops and businesses that I'd driven past daily for almost six weeks melted into a monotonous blur. I had memorized this road and barely had to concentrate on maneuvering it. My mind was free to worry.

So much to do with only two days left

until Christmas. I checked my mental list: Mail Aunt Ellen's package. Shop for the boys. Wrap Mom and Dad's presents.

Cameron shouted from his car seat behind me, bringing my mind back to the present. "Mommy, I wanna see that Santa!"

I glanced to the side of the road, and there sat the same Santa we had driven past for weeks now, waving and smiling the same bearded smile.

"Cameron, I have to do some shopping at the North Valley Plaza. There's probably a Santa out there for you to see," I told him.

"I don't want that Santa Claus—I wanna see this Santa!" Cameron protested.

"OK, OK, I'll try to get over." Anything to keep him quiet, I thought. I have so much to do this afternoon, I don't need a screaming kid on my hands.

I tried to weave into the right lane to go around the block but I couldn't get over. I tried for several blocks and still didn't manage it. "What is this?" I thought. "The traffic is never this bad at this time of the day." Finally, I gave up.

"Cameron, I couldn't get over. We'll have to see the Santa at the mall." Cameron wailed all the way to the mall. I couldn't take it any longer.

"Cameron, hush up!" I scolded, but even

as I yelled it, I felt guilty. I glanced at him in the rear-view mirror.

"Poor little guy," I thought. "He's as pale as a ghost and looks a sight with his hair almost gone."

I wondered about the results of our doctor's last effort to radiate away a second cancerous brain tumor in Cameron's small head. They didn't want to attempt a second surgery on someone so young—he was only 18 months when he'd had the first surgery. Oh, how we had rejoiced when they said they'd "got it all." We had hoped, held our breath, prayed, and hoped some more for two long years. Then, just six weeks before Christmas 1986 we learned that the tumor had grown again.

Although my hopes dwindled, I knew we had to keep fighting it. When the doctors suggested radiation treatment we agreed, even though it would mean an hour and a half daily drive to a larger city for six weeks up to Christmas Day. The drive, stress, and worry were draining me, even as the radiation drained the life from Cameron's once-pink cheeks.

I knew I should be praying instead of worrying. As I parked the car and unstrapped Cameron's car seat, I prayed a quick prayer.

"Lord, I know I should be praying more for Cameron," I confessed. "But with Christmas only two days away, my mind is cluttered with too much to do. I just can't seem to stop. Please understand."

I entered the mall with a heavy heart. The sounds, sights, and smells of Christmas were everywhere. The Salvation Army bell was ringing. Carols were playing softly in the background. Package-laden people were rushing here and there—some tense, some laughing; colored lights were flashing. Chocolate fudge was cooling on the counter of a candy store.

"Christmas is everywhere but in my heart," I thought, as we stepped to the end of the line waiting to see Santa.

The long line moved slowly. Children whined and mothers grew impatient. I clutched Cameron's cool, small hand, gazing at him wistfully, wishing away the whiteness of his skin. He was stretching his neck for a better view and had an expectant gleam in his eyes. We were almost up to Santa!

Finally, it was our turn. Cameron scrambled up into the ornate, cherry-red sleigh and looked up into Santa's face with anticipation. I stood off to the side and watched.

"Well, what do we have here?" Santa

asked, noticing Cameron's balding head. "Are you going to have an operation, son?"

"No, he's having radiation for a brain tumor," I answered from where I stood.

"Come over here, mom," Santa called. I stepped nearer to hear him. "You know that after the doctors have done all they can with their technology, the ultimate healing is up the Lord."

"Oh, absolutely!" I agreed.

"Would you sit up here with me, Mom, and do you mind if I pray for this little guy?"

I shook my head and climbed up into the sleigh next to Cameron.

Santa continued, "I had a serious problem in my brain at one time and the Lord healed me. I believe he will heal Cameron, too."

Santa pulled Cameron and me close, and I felt as if God had reached down and wrapped me up in a warm hug. I needed it so badly right at that moment.

Santa prayed, "Father, in the name of Jesus, I ask you to touch this little fella from the top of his head to the bottom of his feet. Lord Jesus, make him feel good for Christmas. Your Word promises us that 'nothing is impossible with God.' We thank you for healing this little child's body. We praise you in Jesus' name. Amen."

When I opened my eyes, about thirty people had gathered around the sleigh, some bewildered, others with knowing looks. I thanked Santa. Then Cameron and I left the mall.

On the ride home, I realized how easily I could have missed that special moment. If it had been up to me, I would have gone to the available Santa. But God had something much better planned.

He had steered me to a Santa whose fur-clad arms God could use to touch me with his concern, whose lips God could use to offer a prayer of hope when I was too weak to pray. God had led my small son and me to a saintly Santa.

Thank you, Lord, for reaching out and touching Cameron and me through your special Santa. And for putting Christmas into our hearts!